**Next Level Marketing Strategies**

This Ebook will provide an overview of next level marketing strategies and techniques that businesses can use to take their marketing efforts to the next level. The module will cover topics such as personalization, interactive content, influencer marketing, data analysis, augmented reality, user-generated content, artificial intelligence, chatbots, video marketing, and omnichannel marketing.

**By the end of this JOURNEY, you will be able to:**

1. Understand the key concepts and benefits of next level marketing.
2. Identify the different strategies and techniques used in next level marketing.
3. Evaluate the effectiveness of different next level marketing approaches.
4. Develop a plan to implement next level marketing strategies in their own business.

## About the Author

Meet Roberto Tan, a digital and affiliate marketing practitioner, who has spent the last few years learning the art of generating passive income without investing large amounts of capital. With a strong background in journalism and media, Robert knows how to create compelling content that resonates with audiences.

As the founder of a thriving YouTube channel that covers topics ranging from travel and entrepreneurship to technology, inspiration, and motivation, Robert is passionate about building a community of like-minded individuals who inspire and support each other in achieving their dreams.

Roberto's career spans across various industries, having worked as a broadcast journalist for seven years at STUDIO 23 and ABS CBN, he also co-anchored a news program (NEWSLIFE) for three years at The People's Television Network Inc.. He has also co-hosted a tech magazine show, BRAND TV aired on GNN, for a season and headed the sales and marketing department of People's Television Network Inc. and radio station Aliw Broadcasting. Additionally, Robert has co-founded a tech start-up and started small businesses in the past, demonstrating his entrepreneurial spirit.

With Roberto's knowledge and guidance, he can help you begin your journey as an affiliate marketing entrepreneur and learn how to earn from home. He is passionate about helping others find their inspiration and motivation to chase their dreams and believes that it's never too late to start.

## I. Introduction to Next Level Marketing

### *What is next level marketing?*

Next level marketing refers to innovative and cutting-edge marketing strategies and techniques that businesses can use to stand out in a crowded marketplace and connect with their customers in more meaningful ways.

Next level marketing involves leveraging the latest technology, data analysis, and creative approaches to create a personalized and immersive customer experience that builds brand awareness, strengthens customer relationships, and drives conversions.

Some key features of next level marketing include personalization, interactive content, influencer marketing, data analysis, augmented reality, user-generated content, artificial intelligence, chatbots, video marketing, and omnichannel marketing.

By incorporating these strategies and techniques into their marketing plans, businesses can differentiate themselves from their competitors, reach new audiences, and achieve their business goals more effectively.

It's essential to stay up to date with the latest trends and developments in next level marketing to provide your clients with the best possible guidance and support.

### Why is next level marketing important?

Next level marketing is important today because the business landscape is more competitive than ever before. With advancements in technology and the rise of e-commerce, businesses must find new and innovative ways to stand out from the crowd and connect with their customers in more meaningful ways.

Customers today have higher expectations than ever before when it comes to the products and services they consume.

They expect personalized experiences, relevant content, and seamless interactions across all channels. To meet these expectations, businesses must leverage the latest marketing strategies and techniques to create a personalized and immersive customer experience that builds brand awareness, strengthens customer relationships, and drives conversions.

Next level marketing is also important because it allows businesses to gain a deeper understanding of their customers through data analysis and tracking. By gathering data on customer behavior and preferences, businesses can create more targeted and effective marketing campaigns that are more likely to resonate with their audience.

Overall, next level marketing is essential for businesses that want to stay ahead of the curve and achieve their business goals in today's fast-paced and constantly evolving marketplace. By adopting innovative marketing strategies and techniques, businesses can differentiate themselves from their competitors, reach new audiences, and achieve sustainable growth over the long term.

### Key trends in next level marketing

There are several key trends in next level marketing that businesses should be aware of to stay ahead of the curve and remain competitive. Here are some of the most important ones:

1.  **Personalization:** Customers today expect personalized experiences, and businesses that can deliver on this front are more likely to build strong customer relationships and drive conversions. Next level marketing involves using customer data to create customized messaging and offers that are tailored to each individual's interests and preferences.

2.  **Influencer marketing:** Influencer marketing has become a key component of next level marketing, as businesses leverage social media influencers and other online personalities to promote their products and services to their followers. This approach can be particularly effective for reaching younger audiences who may be more skeptical of traditional advertising methods.

3.  **Data analysis:** With the rise of big data and analytics tools, businesses have more opportunities than ever before to gather data on customer behavior and preferences. Next level marketing involves using this data to gain insights into what customers want and

need and using that information to inform marketing strategy and messaging.

4. **Artificial intelligence:** Artificial intelligence is increasingly being used in next level marketing, particularly for chatbots and other customer service applications. AI-powered chatbots can provide customers with quick and personalized responses to their questions and concerns, improving the overall customer experience.

5. **Interactive content:** Interactive content, such as quizzes, polls, and surveys, can be a powerful tool for engaging customers and gathering data. Next level marketing involves using these types of interactive content to create more engaging and memorable experiences for customers.

6. **Video marketing:** Video has become an increasingly popular form of content in recent years, and businesses that incorporate video into their marketing strategies are more likely to engage and retain customers. Next level marketing involves using video to tell compelling brand stories, showcase products and services, and connect with audiences on an emotional level.

7. **Social media:** Social media platforms continue to play a crucial role in next level marketing, providing businesses with a powerful tool for reaching and engaging with their target audience. With the ability

6

to create highly targeted ads and sponsored content, businesses can use social media to reach their ideal customers and build brand awareness.

8. **Voice search optimization:** As more and more people use voice assistants like Siri and Alexa to search for information, businesses that optimize their content for voice search are more likely to be found by potential customers. Next level marketing involves using natural language keywords and phrases in website content and marketing materials to ensure they are optimized for voice search.

9. **Customer experience:** In today's competitive business environment, customer experience is more important than ever before. Next level marketing involves creating a seamless and enjoyable experience for customers at every touchpoint, from initial awareness through to post-purchase follow-up and support.

10. **Sustainability and social responsibility:** Increasingly, customers are looking to do business with companies that prioritize sustainability and social responsibility. Next level marketing involves highlighting a business's commitment to these values in its messaging and marketing materials and integrating them into the overall brand identity.

By staying up to date with these key trends in next level marketing, businesses can create more effective and engaging marketing strategies that drive results and help them achieve their business goals.

Incorporating innovative approaches like personalization, influencer marketing, data analysis, artificial intelligence, and more, businesses can differentiate themselves from their competitors and create a memorable and impactful brand experience for their customers.

## II. Personalization

### *What is personalization and why is it important?*

Personalization is the process of tailoring marketing messages, products, and services to the specific needs, interests, and preferences of individual customers. This can include things like sending targeted emails based on browsing behavior, recommending products based on past purchases, or providing personalized content based on a customer's demographic information.

Personalization is important for several reasons. First and foremost, customers today expect personalized experiences, and businesses that can deliver on this front are more likely to build strong customer relationships and drive conversions. Personalization can help to create a sense of connection and trust between a business and its customers and can make customers feel valued and appreciated.

This can also help businesses to stand out from their competitors. By delivering targeted messages and offers that are tailored to everyone's interests and preferences, businesses can differentiate themselves from others in their

8

industry and create a unique and memorable brand experience for their customers.

Finally, personalization can help businesses to gather data on customer behavior and preferences. By tracking things like website visits, purchasing behavior, and social media engagement, businesses can gain insights into what their customers want and need, and use that information to inform their marketing strategy and messaging.

### How to use customer data to create personalized marketing messages

Using customer data to create personalized marketing messages is an essential part of next level marketing. By tailoring your messaging to everyone's interests and preferences, you can create a more engaging and effective marketing campaign that drives results and builds long-term customer relationships.

Here are some steps you can take to use customer data to create personalized marketing messages:

1. **Collect customer data:** The first step in creating personalized marketing messages is to collect customer data. This can include information like demographics, purchasing behavior, website visits, social media engagement, and more. There are a variety of tools and platforms you can use to collect customer data, including customer relationship management (CRM) software, social media analytics tools, and web analytics platforms.

2. **Segment your audience:** Once you have collected customer data, the next step is to segment your audience based on shared characteristics and behaviors. This can include things like age, gender, location, purchasing behavior, and more. By segmenting your audience, you can create targeted messaging that speaks directly to the needs and interests of each group.

3. **Create personalized messaging:** Once you have segmented your audience, the next step is to create personalized messaging that speaks directly to the needs and interests of each group. This can include things like personalized email campaigns, targeted social media ads, and customized website content. Use the data you have collected to create messaging that resonates with each group and highlight the benefits of your product or service that are most relevant to their needs.

4. **Test and refine:** As with any marketing campaign, it's important to test and refine your messaging over time. Use A/B testing and other techniques to see which messaging is most effective and adjust as needed to improve your results.

5. **Use dynamic content:** Dynamic content is content that changes based on the interests and behaviors of the individual viewing it. For example, you might show different product recommendations to different customers based on their past purchases or browsing

history. Use dynamic content to create a more personalized experience for your customers and increase engagement.

6. **Leverage personalization in your email campaigns:** Email is a powerful tool for personalized marketing. Use customer data to create targeted email campaigns that speak directly to everyone's interests and needs. This can include things like personalized subject lines, customized email content, and targeted offers and promotions.

7. **Create personalized retargeting campaigns:** Retargeting is the practice of showing ads to people who have previously interacted with your brand. Use customer data to create personalized retargeting campaigns that show targeted messaging and offers to each individual based on their past behavior.

8. **Use social media targeting:** Social media platforms like Facebook and Instagram allow you to target your ads to specific audiences based on demographics, interests, and behaviors. Use customer data to create targeted social media campaigns that reach the right people with the right messaging.

9. **Consider using AI and machine learning:** AI and machine learning tools can help you analyze customer data and create personalized messaging at scale. Use these tools to automate your marketing campaigns

and deliver customized messaging to everyone in your audience.

By using customer data to create personalized marketing messages, you can build strong customer relationships, differentiate yourself from your competitors, and drive sustainable growth over the long term.

Just remember to collect data ethically and in accordance with relevant laws and regulations, and always prioritize the privacy and security of your customers' information.

### *Examples of successful personalized marketing campaigns*

Here are five examples of successful personalized international marketing campaigns:

1. **Spotify's Wrapped Campaign:** Every year, Spotify releases its Wrapped campaign, which shows users their top songs, artists, and genres from the past year. This campaign is highly personalized, showing each individual user the music, they listened to most. By creating personalized content that resonates with each user's interests, Spotify is able to engage its audience and build long-term customer loyalty.

2. **Coca-Cola's "Share a Coke" Campaign:** In this campaign, Coca-Cola replaced its traditional logo with popular names and phrases. This personalized touch encouraged customers to purchase bottles of Coca-Cola with their own names on them or the names of friends and family. The campaign was a huge success, leading to increased sales and customer engagement.

3. **Amazon's Personalized Product Recommendations:** Amazon uses customer data to create personalized product recommendations for each individual user. By analyzing past purchases, browsing behavior, and search history, Amazon can show each user products that are relevant to their interests and needs. This personalized approach has helped Amazon become one of the most successful e-commerce companies in the world.

4. **Netflix's Recommendation Algorithm:** Netflix's recommendation algorithm is a prime example of personalized marketing. By analyzing each user's viewing history, Netflix is able to recommend movies and TV shows that are likely to be of interest to each individual user. This personalized approach has helped Netflix become one of the most popular streaming services in the world.

5. **Nike's Personalized Training Plans:** Nike offers personalized training plans through its Nike Training Club app. By asking users to input their fitness goals, interests, and availability, Nike is able to create customized workout plans that are tailored to each individual's needs. This personalized approach has helped Nike build a loyal customer base and increase sales of its fitness products.

Here are five examples of successful personalized marketing campaigns from the Philippines:

1. **Jollibee's "My Jollibee" Campaign: Jollibee**, one of the largest fast-food chains in the Philippines, launched a personalized marketing campaign in 2019 called "My Jollibee." The campaign encouraged customers to share their own stories and memories of Jollibee using the hashtag #MyJollibee. Jollibee then used these stories to create personalized content that resonated with each individual customer.

2. **Lazada's Personalized Shopping Experience:** Lazada, one of the largest e-commerce platforms in the Philippines, uses customer data to create a personalized shopping experience. By analyzing each user's search history and purchasing behavior, Lazada is able to recommend products that are tailored to each individual's interests and needs.

3. **Globe Telecom's Rewards Program:** Globe Telecom, one of the largest telecommunications companies in the Philippines, offers a personalized rewards program for its customers. The program offers personalized rewards based on each customer's usage behavior, allowing Globe Telecom to create a more engaging and relevant customer experience.

4. **Nestle's "Nescafe Moments" Campaign:** Nestle's Nescafe brand launched a personalized marketing campaign in 2019 called "Nescafe Moments." The

campaign used Facebook Messenger to ask customers a series of questions about their coffee preferences, and then recommended personalized coffee recipes based on their answers. This campaign helped Nestle engage with its audience and build brand loyalty.

5. **Cebu Pacific's Personalized Offers:** Cebu Pacific, one of the largest airlines in the Philippines, uses customer data to create personalized flight offers. By analyzing each user's search history and booking behavior, Cebu Pacific is able to offer personalized flight deals that are tailored to each individual's needs and interests.

These examples show that personalized marketing is just as effective in the Philippines as it is in other parts of the world. By tailoring your messaging to everyone's interests and preferences, you can create a more effective marketing campaign that resonates with your audience and builds long-term customer relationships.

## III. Interactive Content

### What is interactive content and why is it important?

Interactive content refers to any form of digital content that requires active engagement from the user. Examples of interactive content include quizzes, polls, surveys, games, interactive infographics, and calculators. Unlike passive content, such as blog posts or videos, interactive content requires the user to take action and provides a more engaging and personalized experience.

15

Interactive content is important for several reasons. First, it helps to capture and maintain the attention of your audience, as it provides a more interesting and engaging experience than static content. This can lead to increased engagement, longer dwell time on your website, and higher levels of brand awareness.

Second, interactive content can help to gather valuable data about your audience. By requiring users to fill out a form, take a quiz, or provide feedback, you can gain insights into their interests, preferences, and behaviors. This information can be used to create more personalized marketing messages and improve the overall customer experience.

Third, interactive content can be highly shareable, as it encourages users to share their results or experiences with others. This can lead to increased reach and brand exposure, as well as higher levels of engagement and user-generated content.

Overall, interactive content is an effective way to engage your audience, gather valuable data, and increase brand awareness. By incorporating interactive content into your marketing strategy, you can create a more personalized and engaging experience for your customers and build stronger relationships with them over time.

*Types of interactive content, such as quizzes, polls, and games*

There are several types of interactive content that you can use in your marketing strategy. Here are a few examples:

1. **Quizzes:** Quizzes are a popular type of interactive content that can be used to engage your audience and educate them about your products or services. Quizzes can be used to test knowledge, personality traits, or product recommendations, among other things.

2. **Polls and Surveys:** Polls and surveys are a great way to gather feedback from your audience and gain insights into their preferences, opinions, and behaviors. They can be used to improve your products, services, or marketing messages.

3. **Interactive Infographics:** Interactive infographics are a visually appealing way to present complex information or data. They can be used to educate your audience and make your content more engaging.

4. **Games:** Games are a fun and engaging way to interact with your audience and keep them on your website for longer periods of time. Games can be used to educate, entertain, or promote products or services.

5. **Calculators:** Calculators can be a useful tool for your audience, especially if you are in a niche that requires complex calculations. For example, a mortgage

calculator can be used by a real estate company to help potential buyers determine how much they can afford to borrow.

6. **Interactive Videos:** Interactive videos are a highly engaging way to interact with your audience. They allow you to create an immersive experience that can be used to educate, entertain, or promote your products or services. Interactive videos can include clickable hotspots, quizzes, and other interactive elements.

7. **Augmented Reality (AR) and Virtual Reality (VR):** AR and VR are powerful tools that can be used to create immersive experiences for your audience. They can be used to showcase products, provide virtual tours, or create engaging games and activities.

8. **Interactive eBooks and Whitepapers:** Interactive eBooks and whitepapers are a great way to create engaging content that can be used to educate your audience about your products or services. They can include interactive elements such as quizzes, videos, and infographics.

9. **Interactive Maps:** Interactive maps can be used to showcase your products or services and provide a more engaging way for your audience to explore your offerings. For example, a travel company could use an interactive map to showcase popular destinations or provide information about local attractions.

10. **Interactive Webinars:** Interactive webinars are a great way to engage your audience and provide valuable information. They can include polls, quizzes, and other interactive elements to keep your audience engaged and interested.

Overall, there are many different types of interactive content that you can use in your marketing strategy. By incorporating interactive elements into your content, you can create a more engaging and personalized experience for your audience, leading to higher engagement, better retention, and increased conversions.

### *Examples of successful interactive content campaigns*

Here are 5 examples of successful INTERNATIONAL interactive content campaigns:

1. **"The Most Stressful Jobs in America" Quiz by CareerBuilder:** CareerBuilder created an interactive quiz that allowed people to find out which job was the most stressful based on their answers to a series of questions. The quiz was a huge success, generating over 1 million views and increasing CareerBuilder's website traffic by 29%.

2. **"The Ultimate Beard Style Guide" by Philips Norelco:** Philips Norelco created an interactive guide that allowed men to choose the perfect beard style based on their facial hair type and personal preferences. The guide was a huge hit, generating over 500,000 views and increasing the company's website traffic by 200%.

3. **"The Interactive Cupcake ATM" by Sprinkles Cupcakes:** Sprinkles Cupcakes created an interactive cupcake ATM that allowed people to order and purchase cupcakes using a touch screen interface. The cupcake ATM was a huge hit, generating significant buzz and increasing foot traffic to Sprinkles Cupcakes locations.

4. **"The World's Smallest IKEA Store" by IKEA**: IKEA created an interactive campaign that allowed people to explore a tiny version of an IKEA store using their smartphones. The campaign was a huge success, generating over 2 million views and increasing the company's social media engagement by 270%.

5. **"The Interactive Pizza Builder" by Pizza Hut:** Pizza Hut created an interactive pizza builder that allowed people to customize their pizza with a variety of toppings and sauces. The campaign was a huge success, generating over 60,000 shares and increasing Pizza Hut's website traffic by 62%.

Here are 5 examples of successful interactive content campaigns in the PHILIPPINES:

1. **"The McDonald's Stripes Run Challenge" by McDonald's**: McDonald's Philippines created an interactive game that challenged people to run as far as they could to win prizes. The game was a huge success, generating significant buzz and increasing engagement on the company's social media pages.

20

2. **"The Jollibee Funko Pop! Challenge" by Jollibee:** Jollibee Philippines created an interactive challenge that encouraged people to collect Jollibee Funko Pop! figures and share their collections on social media. The campaign was a huge success, generating over 500,000 social media posts and increasing the company's social media engagement by 120%.

3. **"The Interactive Kalesa Ride" by Intramuros Administration:** Intramuros Administration created an interactive campaign that allowed people to explore the historic walled city of Intramuros on a virtual kalesa ride. The campaign was a huge success, generating significant buzz and increasing the number of visitors to Intramuros.

4. **"The Globe VR Campaign" by Globe Telecom:** Globe Telecom created an interactive campaign that allowed people to experience different virtual reality scenarios using a VR headset. The campaign was a huge success, generating significant buzz and increasing the company's social media engagement by 150%.

5. **"The Interactive Adobo Recipe Builder" by Ajinomoto:** Ajinomoto Philippines created an interactive adobo recipe builder that allowed people to customize their adobo recipe using different ingredients and cooking methods. The campaign was a huge success, generating over 100,000 social media shares and increasing the company's website traffic by 50%.

By creating content that is fun, interactive, and personalized, you can create a memorable experience for your audience that will drive conversions and loyalty.

## IV. Influencer Marketing

### *What is influencer marketing and why is it important?*

Influencer marketing is a type of marketing that involves partnering with influential individuals on social media platforms to promote a brand, product, or service. These influencers have a large following on social media, and they can reach a highly engaged audience with their content.

Influencer marketing is important because it allows brands to reach their target audience in an authentic and engaging way. By partnering with influencers who have a similar target audience, brands can leverage the trust and credibility that these influencers have built with their followers to increase brand awareness, drive sales, and build brand loyalty.

In addition, influencer marketing allows brands to tap into the power of social media and reach a wider audience than traditional marketing methods. With the rise of social media platforms, people are increasingly turning to influencers for product recommendations and advice, making influencer marketing an effective way to connect with consumers and build brand awareness.

### How to identify and partner with social media influencers

As social media continues to grow and evolve, influencer marketing has become a crucial part of many brands' marketing strategies. Influencers have built up loyal followings that trust their recommendations and opinions, making them valuable partners for brands looking to reach new audiences.

Here's how to best identify and partner with social media influencers:

1. **Define your campaign goals:** Before you start searching for influencers, it's important to define the goals of your influencer marketing campaign. Are you looking to increase brand awareness, drive sales, or build brand loyalty? Having clear goals in mind will help you find the right influencers to partner with.

2. **Identify your target audience:** Knowing your target audience is critical for finding influencers who can reach them effectively. Consider demographics such as age, gender, location, and interests to identify the social media platforms your target audience is most active on.

3. **Research potential influencers:** Use social media platforms and influencer marketing tools to research potential influencers. Look for influencers with a large following, high engagement rate, and content that resonates with your target audience. Also, consider

23

the influencer's reputation and whether they align with your brand values.

4. **Evaluate potential influencers:** Evaluate potential influencers based on factors such as their audience demographics, engagement rates, authenticity, and relevance to your brand. You can also look at their past campaigns and collaborations to see if they align with your brand's values.

5. **Reach out to influencers:** Reach out to the influencers you've identified with a personalized message that outlines your goals and why you think they would be a good fit for your brand. Be clear about the benefits of the partnership for both parties, and be open to negotiation.

6. **Collaborate with influencers:** If an influencer agrees to work with you, collaborate with them to create a campaign that aligns with your goals and their content style. Provide them with clear guidelines and resources to create high-quality content that promotes your brand.

7. **Monitor and measure results:** Monitor and measure the results of your influencer marketing campaign using analytics tools to track engagement rates, reach, conversions, and other metrics. Use the data to adjust your strategy and optimize results for future campaigns.

By following these steps, you can identify the right social media influencers to partner with and create a successful influencer marketing campaign that helps you reach new audiences and achieve your business goals.

*Examples of successful influencer marketing campaigns*

Here are 5 examples of successful international influencer marketing campaigns:

1. **Daniel Wellington's #DWPickoftheDay Campaign:** Daniel Wellington, a watch brand, partnered with Instagram influencers to promote their watches using the hashtag #DWPickoftheDay. The campaign generated over 1.5 million posts and helped the brand reach new audiences and increase sales.

2. **Coca-Cola's #ShareaCoke Campaign:** Coca-Cola's #ShareaCoke campaign encouraged customers to share a Coke with a friend or family member and featured personalized Coke bottles with people's names on them. The brand also partnered with influencers to promote the campaign on social media, which helped it reach a wider audience and generate buzz.

3. **H&M's Coachella Campaign:** H&M partnered with social media influencers to promote their clothing line at the Coachella music festival. The influencers shared photos and videos of themselves wearing H&M outfits, which helped the brand generate a lot of buzz and reach a younger audience.

25

4. **Glossier's #BoyBrow Campaign:** Glossier, a beauty brand, partnered with influencers to promote their #BoyBrow eyebrow product. The influencers shared photos and videos of themselves using the product, which helped the brand reach a wider audience and generate buzz.

5. **McDonald's McDelivery Night In Campaign:** McDonald's partnered with social media influencers to promote their McDelivery service, which allowed customers to order food delivery from McDonald's. The influencers shared photos and videos of themselves having a "night in" with McDonald's food, which helped the brand reach a wider audience and increase sales.

Here are 5 examples of successful influencer marketing campaigns in the Philippines:

1. **Colgate's #SmileStrong Campaign:** Colgate partnered with social media influencers to promote their #SmileStrong campaign, which aimed to encourage Filipinos to be confident and show off their smiles. The influencers shared photos and videos of themselves using Colgate products and showing off their smiles, which helped the brand generate buzz and increase sales.

2. **Jollibee's #KwentongJollibee Valentine's Day Campaign:** Jollibee, a fast-food chain, partnered with social media influencers to promote their #KwentongJollibee Valentine's Day campaign, which

26

featured heartwarming stories about love and relationships. The influencers shared their own stories and encouraged their followers to share theirs, which helped the brand generate a lot of buzz and increase sales.

3. **Lazada's 11.11 Shopping Festival:** Lazada, an e-commerce platform, partnered with social media influencers to promote their 11.11 shopping festival, which offered discounts and deals on a wide range of products. The influencers shared photos and videos of themselves shopping on Lazada and promoting the deals, which helped the brand generate a lot of buzz and increase sales.

4. **Olay's #FaceAnything Campaign:** Olay partnered with social media influencers to promote their #FaceAnything campaign, which aimed to encourage women to be confident and overcome their insecurities. The influencers shared photos and videos of themselves using Olay products and sharing their own stories of overcoming challenges, which helped the brand generate buzz and increase sales.

5. **Globe Telecom's #CreateCourage Campaign:** Globe Telecom partnered with social media influencers to promote their #CreateCourage campaign, which aimed to encourage Filipinos to be courageous and pursue their passions. The influencers shared their own stories and encouraged their followers to do the

same, which helped the brand generate a lot of buzz and increase engagement on social media.

These campaigns were successful because they partnered with influencers who had a large following and a strong influence on their audience. The influencers helped the brands reach new audiences and generate buzz, which led to increased sales and brand awareness.

## V. Data Analysis

### *What is data analysis and why is it important?*

Data analysis is the process of systematically examining and interpreting data to extract meaningful insights and draw conclusions. It involves collecting, cleaning, organizing, and analyzing data to identify patterns, trends, and relationships that can inform business decisions.

Data analysis is important because it helps businesses make informed decisions based on empirical evidence rather than intuition or guesswork. By analyzing data, businesses can identify opportunities, assess risks, measure performance, and evaluate the effectiveness of their strategies and tactics. It can also help businesses optimize their operations, improve their products or services, and increase their competitiveness in the marketplace.

In today's data-driven business environment, data analysis has become an essential tool for businesses of all sizes and industries. With the increasing availability of data and the emergence of new technologies such as machine learning and artificial intelligence, data analysis is more important than ever for businesses that want to stay ahead of the competition and succeed in the long term.

***How to collect and analyze customer data to improve marketing efforts***

Collecting and analyzing customer data is crucial for improving marketing efforts and achieving business success. Here are some steps to collect and analyze customer data to improve marketing efforts:

1. **Identify Data Needs:** The first step is to identify what data is needed to achieve marketing goals. This involves setting objectives and determining what data needs to be collected to meet these objectives. For example, a business may want to collect data on customer demographics, preferences, behavior, and purchase history to better understand their target audience.

2. **Choose Data Collection Methods:** There are several methods for collecting customer data, including surveys, interviews, customer feedback, social media monitoring, and website analytics. It is important to choose the right method based on the objectives of the analysis, the target audience, and the type of data being collected.

3. **Collect and Store Data:** Once the data collection method is chosen, the next step is to collect and store the data. It is important to ensure that the data is

29

accurate, complete, and secure. Businesses can use data management tools such as customer relationship management (CRM) software to store and manage customer data.

4. **Clean and Organize Data:** After collecting data, it needs to be cleaned and organized. This involves removing irrelevant or duplicate data and structuring it in a way that makes it easy to analyze. Businesses can use data cleansing and structuring tools to simplify this process.

5. **Analyze Data:** The next step is to analyze the data to gain insights into customer behavior and preferences. This involves using statistical analysis techniques, data visualization tools, or machine learning algorithms to identify patterns and trends in the data.

6. **Interpret Results:** After analyzing the data, the results need to be interpreted to gain actionable insights. This involves identifying the key takeaways from the analysis and determining how they can be applied to improve marketing efforts. For example, if data shows that a majority of customers prefer a specific product feature, the business can use this insight to improve product development and marketing messaging.

7. **Implement Changes:** Based on the insights gained from the analysis, businesses can implement changes to improve their marketing efforts. This could involve

changing marketing messaging, targeting specific customer segments, or adjusting marketing channels.

8. **Monitor and Measure Results:** Finally, it is important to monitor and measure the impact of the changes made to ensure that they are effective. This involves tracking key performance indicators such as customer acquisition, retention, and conversion rates, and making further adjustments if necessary.

In summary, collecting and analyzing customer data is a continuous process that involves identifying data needs, choosing data collection methods, collecting and storing data, cleaning and organizing data, analyzing data, interpreting results, implementing changes, and monitoring and measuring results. By following these steps, businesses can gain valuable insights into their customers and improve their marketing efforts to achieve business success.

*Examples of successful data-driven marketing campaigns*

Here are the top 5 International examples of successful data-driven marketing campaigns:

1. **Amazon - Recommendation system:** Amazon uses customer data to power its recommendation system, which suggests products to customers based on their past purchases and browsing history. This has resulted in increased customer loyalty and repeat purchases, as well as higher revenue for the company.

2. **Coca-Cola - "Share a Coke" campaign:** Coca-Cola used customer data to create a personalized marketing campaign, where the brand replaced its logo with popular names and nicknames on its bottles and cans. This led to increased social media engagement and sales.

3. **Netflix - Content recommendations**: Netflix uses customer data to recommend TV shows and movies to its subscribers based on their viewing history and preferences. This has resulted in increased customer satisfaction and retention.

4. **Nike - Nike Plus app:** Nike collects data on its customers' fitness activities and uses that information to provide personalized workout plans and training tips through its Nike Plus app. This has resulted in increased customer engagement and loyalty.

5. **Spotify - Personalized playlists: Spotify** uses customer data to create personalized playlists for its users based on their listening history and preferences. This has resulted in increased user engagement and retention for the music streaming service.

Overall, successful data-driven marketing campaigns use customer data to create a personalized experience for each individual customer.

By tailoring marketing efforts to each customer's preferences and needs, companies can increase customer engagement, retention, and loyalty.

## VI. Augmented Reality

### *What is augmented reality and why is it important?*

Augmented reality (AR) is a technology that overlays digital information onto the real world, creating a blended experience for the user. AR is different from virtual reality (VR), which creates an entirely digital world for the user to inhabit. With AR, users can experience digital elements as if they are part of the real world around them.

AR is important in marketing because it provides a unique and immersive experience for customers. By incorporating AR into marketing campaigns, companies can create engaging and interactive experiences that capture customers' attention and leave a lasting impression.

One example of AR in marketing is the use of virtual try-on technology in the beauty industry. Customers can use their smartphones to see what different shades of lipstick or eyeshadow would look like on their face before making a purchase. This creates a personalized and engaging shopping experience that is tailored to each individual customer.

Another example is the use of AR in the automotive industry. Car manufacturers can use AR to allow customers to visualize how different features would look on a car, such as different colors or wheel options. This creates a more interactive and engaging car shopping experience that can help customers make a more informed purchase decision.

AR is also becoming more prevalent in the retail industry, with companies using AR to create virtual stores or

33

interactive displays. For example, IKEA has an AR app that allows customers to see what furniture would look like in their home before making a purchase.

Overall, AR provides a new and innovative way for companies to engage with customers and create memorable experiences. By incorporating AR into marketing campaigns, companies can differentiate themselves from competitors and create a more personalized and immersive experience for customers.

### *How to use AR to create immersive experiences for customers*

Augmented Reality (AR) technology offers a unique opportunity for marketers to create immersive experiences for customers that blend the physical and digital worlds.

Here are some steps for using AR to create engaging and interactive marketing campaigns:

1. **Determine the objective of the campaign:** Before diving into creating an AR campaign, it's important to determine the objective of the campaign. Is the goal to increase brand awareness, drive sales, or provide a unique customer experience? Understanding the objective will help guide the creative process and ensure the campaign is aligned with business goals.

2. **Identify the target audience:** It's important to understand the target audience for the campaign, as this will impact the type of AR experience that is created. For example, an AR campaign targeting

children will have different requirements and design elements than one targeting adults.

3. **Choose the AR platform:** There are many different AR platforms available, ranging from mobile apps to browser-based experiences. Choose a platform that aligns with the objectives of the campaign and the target audience.

4. **Create engaging content:** Once the platform has been chosen, it's time to create the content for the AR experience. This could be anything from interactive product demonstrations to virtual games or immersive storytelling.

5. **Test and refine the experience:** It's important to test the AR experience with a small group of users before launching it to a wider audience. This will help identify any technical or user experience issues and allow for refinements to be made before the campaign goes live.

6. **Launch the campaign:** Once the AR experience has been refined and tested, it's time to launch the campaign. This can be done through social media, email marketing, or other digital channels.

7. **Analyze the results:** After the campaign has run, it's important to analyze the results to determine its effectiveness. This could include metrics such as engagement, reach, and conversion rates. This

analysis will help inform future AR campaigns and improve marketing efforts.

Overall, AR offers a unique opportunity for marketers to create engaging and immersive experiences for customers. By following these steps, companies can leverage AR technology to differentiate themselves from competitors, drive sales, and create memorable experiences for customers.

### Top 10 AR Platforms available

Here are the top 10 AR platforms and a brief explanation of each:

1.  **ARCore by Google:** ARCore is an AR platform that uses machine learning to understand the environment and create AR experiences. It is compatible with Android devices.

2.  **ARKit by Apple:** ARKit is a toolkit that enables developers to build AR apps for Apple devices using features such as motion tracking, environmental understanding, and light estimation.

3.  **Vuforia:** Vuforia is an AR platform that uses computer vision to recognize and track images and objects in the real world, enabling AR experiences to be overlaid on them.

4.  **Wikitude:** Wikitude is an AR platform that supports marker-based and markerless AR, and allows developers to create location-based AR experiences.

5. **Unity:** Unity is a game engine that includes built-in support for AR development. It supports multiple platforms, including iOS, Android, and Windows.

6. **ZapWorks:** ZapWorks is an AR platform that allows users to create AR experiences using drag-and-drop tools and JavaScript. It supports marker-based and markerless AR.

7. **MAXST:** MAXST is an AR platform that supports both marker-based and markerless AR, and includes features such as 3D object tracking and image recognition.

8. **EasyAR:** EasyAR is an AR platform that supports both marker-based and markerless AR, and includes features such as cloud recognition and face tracking.

9. **8th Wall:** 8th Wall is an AR platform that allows developers to create web-based AR experiences that can be accessed through a mobile browser.

10. **Spark AR Studio by Facebook:** Spark AR Studio is an AR platform that allows users to create AR effects for Facebook and Instagram. It includes features such as face tracking and object recognition.

Each of these platforms has its own strengths and weaknesses, and the best one for a particular project will depend on factors such as the target audience, the type of AR experience being developed, and the resources available.

*Examples of successful AR marketing campaigns*

Here are some examples of successful AR marketing campaigns Internationally:

1. **Pepsi Max's Unbelievable Bus Shelter: In** 2014, Pepsi Max launched an AR campaign at a bus shelter in London. The shelter was fitted with a digital screen that displayed various scenes, such as an alien invasion and a tiger running loose. However, when people looked at the screen through the camera of their smartphone, they saw additional content that wasn't visible to the naked eye. The campaign generated over 6 million views on YouTube and was a hit on social media.

2. **IKEA Place:** IKEA's AR app, IKEA Place, lets customers virtually place furniture in their homes before making a purchase. By using their smartphone camera, customers can see how a piece of furniture would look in their space in real-time. The app has been praised for its accuracy and ease of use.

3. **Sephora Virtual Artist:** Sephora's AR app, Virtual Artist, allows customers to try on makeup virtually. Users can upload a photo of themselves or use their smartphone camera to see how different shades of lipstick, eyeshadow, and other products would look on their face. The app has been a hit with customers and has helped increase Sephora's online sales.

4. **NBA AR Game:** The NBA partnered with Snapchat to launch an AR game that allowed users to play a virtual game of basketball on their smartphone. The game used AR technology to place a virtual hoop in the real world, and users had to use their finger to flick a virtual basketball into the hoop. The campaign was a hit on social media and helped drive engagement with the NBA brand.

5. **Hyundai Virtual Guide:** In 2016, Hyundai launched an AR app called the Hyundai Virtual Guide. The app provides customers with a virtual owner's manual, allowing them to use their smartphone camera to identify and learn about various features in their car. The app has been praised for its user-friendliness and has helped improve customer satisfaction with the Hyundai brand.

6. **McDonald's AR Coloring Book:** McDonald's Brazil launched an AR coloring book that allowed kids to bring their coloring pages to life using AR technology. When a child finished coloring a page, they could use the McDonald's app to scan the page and see their artwork come to life in 3D. The campaign was a hit with parents and children and helped increase brand engagement with the McDonald's brand.

Here are some examples of successful AR marketing campaigns in the Philippines:

1. **Coca-Cola Philippines' "Taste the Feeling" Campaign** - In 2016, Coca-Cola Philippines launched an AR campaign that allowed customers to scan their Coke cans or bottles with their mobile devices to unlock virtual Coke emoticons that they could share on social media.

2. **McDonald's Philippines' "McDonald's AR Adventures"** - McDonald's Philippines launched an AR campaign in 2018 that featured interactive games that customers could play using their mobile devices. The games were accessible through the McDonald's mobile app and featured McDonald's mascots.

3. **Nestlé Philippines' "Create Your Break AR Campaign"** - In 2019, Nestlé Philippines launched an AR campaign that allowed customers to create their own virtual breaks using their mobile devices. Customers could scan a Nestlé product and access the AR experience, which featured relaxing scenes like the beach or the countryside.

4. **Jollibee Philippines' "AR Game with Jollibee and Friends"** - In 2020, Jollibee Philippines launched an AR game that customers could access through the Jollibee mobile app. The game featured Jollibee and his friends

These are just a few examples of successful AR marketing campaigns. Each campaign used AR technology in a unique way to create an immersive and engaging experience for customers.

## VII. User-Generated Content

### *What is user-generated content and why is it important?*

User-generated content (UGC) refers to any content created by users, customers, or fans that is publicly available for others to view, share, or engage with. This can include social media posts, reviews, photos, videos, and more. UGC is important in marketing because it provides authentic and genuine content that can help build trust with potential customers.

One of the main benefits of UGC is that it provides social proof, which is a psychological phenomenon where people rely on the opinions and actions of others to guide their own behavior. When potential customers see that others are using and enjoying a product or service, they are more likely to trust and engage with that brand. UGC can also help to humanize a brand, making it more relatable and personable to customers.

Another benefit of UGC is that it can help to fill gaps in a brand's content strategy. Creating high-quality content can be time-consuming and costly, but UGC provides a free and readily available source of content that can be repurposed and shared across various marketing channels.

To effectively leverage UGC in marketing, brands must first identify and encourage their customers to create and

41

share content. This can be done through social media campaigns, contests, and incentivized programs. Brands can also monitor social media channels and review sites to find and curate relevant UGC.

Once UGC is collected, it can be repurposed and shared across various marketing channels, such as social media, email campaigns, and website content. Brands can also engage with users who have created UGC by commenting, liking, and sharing their content, which can help to build stronger relationships with customers.

Overall, UGC is an important and valuable tool in marketing that can help build trust with potential customers, humanize a brand, and fill gaps in a brand's content strategy. By identifying and encouraging customers to create and share content, brands can leverage UGC to drive engagement and ultimately, increase sales.

### How to encourage customers to create and share content about your brand

Encouraging customers to create and share content about your brand is an effective way to leverage user-generated content (UGC) in your marketing strategy.

Here are some tips on how to encourage customers to create and share content about your brand:

1. **Create a branded hashtag:** A branded hashtag can encourage customers to share their experiences with your brand on social media. Make sure the hashtag is short, catchy, and easy to remember.

2. **Run a UGC contest:** A UGC contest can incentivize customers to create and share content about your brand. Offer a prize or reward for the best submission, and make sure to promote the contest on your social media channels.

3. **Showcase UGC on your website and social media channels:** Highlighting UGC on your website and social media channels can encourage others to share their experiences with your brand. Make sure to ask for permission before sharing UGC and give proper credit to the creator.

4. **Collaborate with influencers:** Partnering with influencers can help you reach a wider audience and encourage UGC. Collaborate with influencers to create content featuring your brand, and encourage their followers to create and share their own content using your branded hashtag.

5. **Offer exclusive experiences:** Offering exclusive experiences or access to events can encourage customers to create and share UGC. Make sure to promote these experiences on your social media channels and encourage attendees to share their experiences using your branded hashtag.

6. **Engage with your audience:** Engaging with your audience on social media can encourage them to create and share UGC. Respond to comments and

messages and ask for feedback on your products or services.

Encouraging customers to create and share content about your brand can help you build a strong community and increase brand awareness. By following these tips, you can leverage the power of UGC in your marketing strategy.

*Examples of successful user-generated content campaigns*

Here are some examples of successful user-generated content international campaigns:

1. **Coca-Cola's "Share a Coke" Campaign:** In this campaign, Coca-Cola replaced its iconic logo with popular names and encouraged customers to find bottles with their names on them and share pictures on social media using the hashtag #ShareACoke. The campaign generated a massive amount of user-generated content and increased Coca-Cola's sales by 2.5%.

2. **Starbucks' "White Cup Contest":** Starbucks invited customers to decorate their plain white cups and share their creations on social media using the hashtag #WhiteCupContest. The winning design was turned into a limited-edition Starbucks cup, and the campaign generated over 4,000 entries in just three weeks.

3. **Airbnb's "One Less Stranger" Campaign:** Airbnb encouraged hosts to perform random acts of kindness for their guests and share their experiences on social

media using the hashtag #OneLessStranger. The campaign generated over 3 million interactions on social media, and Airbnb reported a 200% increase in the number of people who signed up to host.

4. **GoPro's "Million Dollar Challenge":** GoPro invited its customers to submit their best GoPro videos for a chance to win a share of a $1 million prize pool. The campaign generated over 25,000 video submissions and increased GoPro's social media following by 6%.

5. **Lay's "Do Us a Flavor" Campaign:** Lay's asked customers to submit their flavor ideas for a chance to win $1 million and have their flavor produced by Lay's. The campaign generated over 3.8 million submissions and increased Lay's sales by 12% in the year following the campaign.

Here are some examples of successful user-generated content campaigns in the Philippines:

1. **Jollibee's #KwentongJollibee Valentine's Day Campaign** - Jollibee, a popular fast-food chain in the Philippines, launched a Valentine's Day campaign called #KwentongJollibee where they asked customers to share their love stories that happened in a Jollibee store. They received thousands of entries and created short films based on the most heartwarming stories. The campaign went viral on social media and helped to strengthen the emotional connection between customers and the brand.

45

2. **Nestle's #KrispiesKarnival Campaign** - Nestle Philippines launched an online contest called #KrispiesKarnival where they asked customers to create their own version of the Nestle Koko Krunch jingle using a karaoke app. The winners received prizes and their jingles were used in Nestle's marketing campaigns. The campaign generated a lot of buzz and engagement on social media.

3. **Globe Telecom's #CreateCourage Campaign** - Globe Telecom, a leading telecommunications company in the Philippines, launched a campaign called #CreateCourage where they asked customers to share their stories of courage and resilience during the COVID-19 pandemic. The entries were compiled into a short film that was shared on social media. The campaign received a positive response and helped to showcase the brand's commitment to its customers.

4. **Havaianas' #MyUrbanBeachStories Campaign** - Havaianas, a popular Brazilian footwear brand, launched a campaign called #MyUrbanBeachStories where they asked customers to share their stories of finding the beach in the city. The entries were shared on social media and the winners received prizes. The campaign helped to create a sense of community and promote the brand's beach lifestyle image.

5. **Smart Communications' #LiveMore Campaign** - Smart Communications, one of the largest mobile network operators in the Philippines, launched a campaign

called #LiveMore where they asked customers to share photos and videos of their memorable experiences using the hashtag #LiveMore. The entries were compiled into a video that was shared on social media. The campaign encouraged customers to live in the moment and connect with the brand's message of empowerment and innovation.

These campaigns show that user-generated content can be a powerful tool in creating engagement and building a stronger relationship between customers and brands. By encouraging customers to share their stories and experiences, brands can tap into the emotional connection that customers have with their products or services.

## VIII. Artificial Intelligence

### *What is artificial intelligence and why is it important?*

Artificial intelligence, or AI, refers to the ability of machines or computer programs to perform tasks that typically require human intelligence, such as learning, problem-solving, decision-making, and pattern recognition. AI involves the use of algorithms, statistical models, and neural networks to analyze vast amounts of data and generate insights that can be used to improve business operations, customer experiences, and marketing strategies.

In the context of marketing, AI can be used to automate and optimize various tasks, such as customer segmentation, lead scoring, personalization, chatbots, and predictive analytics. It can also be used to enhance the customer experience by providing personalized recommendations, predicting customer behavior, and improving response times.

AI is important in next level marketing because it enables businesses to make more informed and data-driven decisions, leading to increased efficiency and effectiveness. With AI, businesses can gain a deeper understanding of their customers' needs and preferences, allowing them to deliver more personalized and relevant experiences.

AI can also help businesses automate repetitive tasks, freeing up time for marketers to focus on more strategic initiatives. Additionally, AI-powered chatbots can provide round-the-clock customer service, improving response times and reducing customer frustration.

Overall, AI is important in next level marketing because it can provide businesses with a competitive edge by enabling them to make better decisions, improve customer experiences, and increase efficiency.

### How to use AI-powered tools to automate marketing tasks and personalize messaging

Using AI-powered tools can help automate tasks and personalize messaging for a better customer experience. Here are the steps to follow to utilize AI-powered tools:

1. **Identify the marketing tasks that can be automated** - Some examples of marketing tasks that can be automated with AI include lead scoring, email

marketing, content creation, social media management, and data analysis.

2. **Choose the right AI-powered tool** - There are many AI-powered tools available, so it's important to choose one that fits your marketing needs. Look for tools that are user-friendly, provide actionable insights, and integrate well with your existing marketing technology stack.

3. **Train the AI tool** - Before you can use an AI-powered tool, you need to train it to recognize patterns and behaviors in your data. This can be done by providing the tool with historical data and setting parameters for it to learn from.

4. **Implement personalized messaging** - Once the AI tool has learned from your data; it can help you create personalized messaging that is tailored to each customer's needs and preferences. For example, you can use AI to create personalized product recommendations, email subject lines, and ad copy.

5. **Continuously analyze and optimize** - AI-powered tools can provide valuable insights into customer behavior and help you optimize your marketing campaigns. Continuously analyze the data provided by the tool and adjust your strategies accordingly to maximize results.

Overall, using AI-powered tools can help you streamline your marketing tasks, deliver more personalized messaging, and ultimately improve the customer experience.

Here are the top 15 trending AI tools available in the market:

1. **OpenAI (https://openai.com/):** An AI research laboratory consisting of the for-profit OpenAI LP and the non-profit OpenAI Inc. The website provides access to a range of AI models and tools for natural language processing, robotics, and more.

2. **TensorFlow (https://www.tensorflow.org/):** A popular open-source machine learning framework developed by Google. It offers a range of tools and resources for building and deploying AI applications.

3. **IBM Watson (https://www.ibm.com/watson):** A suite of AI tools and services developed by IBM. The website provides access to APIs and tools for natural language processing, speech recognition, image analysis, and more.

4. **Microsoft Azure AI (https://azure.microsoft.com/en-us/services/cognitive-services/):** A cloud-based platform for building and deploying AI applications. The website offers access to a range of AI tools and services, including speech and image recognition, natural language processing, and more.

5. **Hugging Face (https://huggingface.co/):** A website that provides access to a range of natural language processing tools and models, including language translation, text classification, and more.

6. **AI Dungeon (https://www.aidungeon.io/):** An AI-powered text adventure game that uses natural language processing to generate a story based on the user's input.

7. **Clarifai (https://www.clarifai.com/):** A website that provides access to a range of AI tools for image and video analysis, including object recognition, facial recognition, and more.

8. **Algorithmia (https://algorithmia.com/):** A website that provides access to a range of AI models and tools for natural language processing, computer vision, and more.

9. **Google Cloud AI (https://cloud.google.com/ai-platform):** A cloud-based platform for building and deploying AI applications. The website offers access to a range of AI tools and services, including natural language processing, speech recognition, and more.

10. **Intel                                              AI (https://www.intel.com/content/www/us/en/artifi cial-intelligence/ai-overview.html):** A website that provides access to a range of AI tools and resources,

including software libraries, hardware, and developer tools.

11. **NVIDIA AI (https://www.nvidia.com/en-us/ai/):** A website that provides access to a range of AI tools and resources, including software libraries, hardware, and developer tools.

12. **KAI (https://www.kai.ai/):** A website that provides access to a range of AI tools and services for building and deploying chatbots.

13. **Wit.ai (https://wit.ai/):** A website that provides access to a natural language processing platform for building chatbots and other AI applications.

14. **SalesForce                                    Einstein (https://www.salesforce.com/products/einstein/ov erview/):** A suite of AI-powered tools and services for customer relationship management, including natural language processing and predictive analytics.

15. **Ayasdi (https://www.ayasdi.com/):** A website that provides access to a range of AI tools and services for healthcare, finance, and other industries. The platform uses machine learning and data analysis to identify patterns and insights in large datasets.

*Examples of successful AI-powered marketing campaigns*

Here are 5 examples of successful AI-powered marketing campaigns:

1. **Sephora:** Sephora used an AI-powered chatbot on the messaging app Kik to help customers find the right makeup products. The chatbot asked customers a series of questions and then provided personalized product recommendations. The campaign was successful in increasing customer engagement and sales.

2. **Spotify:** Spotify uses AI algorithms to provide personalized recommendations to its users. By analyzing user listening data, Spotify can suggest new songs and artists that users are likely to enjoy. This has been a successful marketing strategy for the company, as it keeps users engaged with the platform and encourages them to continue using the service.

3. **Coca-Cola:** Coca-Cola used AI-powered vending machines to create a personalized marketing experience for customers. The vending machines used facial recognition technology to detect customers' gender and age, and then provided them with targeted product recommendations. This campaign was successful in increasing customer engagement and brand awareness.

4. **McDonald's:** McDonald's used AI-powered digital menu boards to create personalized recommendations for customers based on factors such as time of day and weather conditions. This campaign was successful in increasing sales and improving customer satisfaction.

Overall, these AI-powered marketing campaigns were successful because they provided personalized recommendations and experiences for customers, which helped to increase engagement and drive sales. By using AI algorithms to analyze customer data, companies can provide more targeted and effective marketing campaigns.

## IX. Chatbots

### *What are chatbots and why are they important?*

Chatbots are computer programs designed to simulate human conversation through text or voice interactions. They use natural language processing and machine learning algorithms to understand and interpret user queries and respond in a conversational manner. Chatbots can be deployed on messaging platforms, mobile apps, websites, and social media platforms.

Chatbots are important for several reasons:

1. **24/7 availability:** Chatbots can operate 24/7, allowing businesses to provide support and assistance to their customers even outside of business hours.

2. **Increased efficiency:** Chatbots can handle multiple customer interactions simultaneously, reducing the workload of customer service representatives and increasing efficiency.

3. **Improved customer experience:** Chatbots provide a personalized and engaging experience for customers, which can lead to increased customer satisfaction and loyalty.

4. **Cost-effective:** Chatbots can reduce the cost of customer support and increase operational efficiency, leading to cost savings for businesses.

5. **Data collection:** Chatbots can collect valuable data about customer preferences, behavior, and needs, which can be used to improve marketing strategies and personalize customer experiences.

Overall, chatbots are an important tool for businesses to improve customer service, increase efficiency, and reduce costs.

### How to use chatbots to provide personalized customer service and generate leads

Chatbots are a useful tool for businesses to provide personalized customer service and generate leads. Here's how to use them effectively:

1. **Define your goals:** Before creating a chatbot, define what you want to achieve with it. Are you looking to provide customer service or generate leads? Having a

clear goal in mind will help you design the chatbot accordingly.

2. **Design a conversation flow:** Map out a conversation flow that your chatbot will follow. This should include the initial greeting, responses to common questions, and call-to-actions to guide users towards your goal.

3. **Personalize the experience:** Use the data you have on your customers to personalize the chatbot experience. For example, use their name in the greeting, offer personalized recommendations based on their past purchases, and address any issues they've had in the past.

4. **Provide value:** Make sure your chatbot provides real value to users. This can be in the form of answering common questions, offering personalized recommendations, or providing relevant information.

5. **Test and optimize:** Once your chatbot is live, test it thoroughly to ensure it's working as intended. Use data and feedback to optimize the conversation flow and improve the user experience over time.

6. **Integrate with other marketing channels:** Use chatbots in conjunction with other marketing channels, such as email and social media, to generate leads and provide a seamless customer experience.

By using chatbots effectively, businesses can provide personalized customer service and generate leads at scale, freeing up valuable time and resources for other areas of the business.

*Examples of successful chatbot-powered marketing campaigns*

Here are 5 top examples of successful chatbot-powered marketing campaigns:

1. **H&M:** H&M's chatbot on the messaging app Kik helped customers find the perfect outfit for their next event by asking questions about their style preferences and providing suggestions based on their answers. The chatbot also had a "shop now" feature that allowed customers to purchase the items directly through the chatbot.

2. **Sephora:** Sephora's chatbot on the messaging app Kik allowed customers to book in-store appointments, view products, and get recommendations on makeup and skincare products. The chatbot also provided personalized beauty tips based on the customer's preferences.

3. **Domino's:** Domino's created a chatbot that allowed customers to order pizza through Facebook Messenger. The chatbot provided customers with a menu of options and allowed them to customize their order, track their delivery, and receive special promotions.

4.  **CNN:** CNN created a chatbot on Facebook Messenger that provided users with news updates and allowed them to personalize the types of news they wanted to receive. Users could also ask the chatbot questions about specific news topics and receive relevant information.

5.  **1-800-Flowers:** 1-800-Flowers created a chatbot on Facebook Messenger that allowed customers to order flowers and gifts, track their delivery, and receive special offers. The chatbot also had a "concierge" feature that allowed customers to ask for gift suggestions based on the recipient's preferences.

Here are 5 examples of successful chatbot-powered marketing campaigns in the Philippines:

1.  **Globe Telecom - Gie the Chatbot:** Globe Telecom launched a chatbot named Gie that was integrated into their website and Facebook page to provide customers with 24/7 assistance. Gie was designed to handle a wide range of customer queries, from bill inquiries to technical support, and was able to resolve over 80% of customer issues. This resulted in a significant reduction in customer service response times and improved customer satisfaction.

2.  **BPI - Bea the Chatbot:** Bank of the Philippine Islands (BPI) launched a chatbot named Bea to assist customers with their banking needs. Bea was able to provide customers with real-time updates on their account balance, transaction history, and even answer

58

frequently asked questions about the bank's products and services. The chatbot was integrated with BPI's mobile banking app and was able to assist customers 24/7.

3. **Jollibee - JoyRide:** Jollibee, a popular fast-food chain in the Philippines, launched a chatbot-powered delivery service named JoyRide. Customers were able to order their favorite meals through Facebook Messenger and track their orders in real-time. The chatbot was able to handle multiple orders at once and was integrated with Jollibee's existing ordering system, resulting in faster delivery times and increased customer satisfaction.

4. **L'Oréal Philippines - Liv:** L'Oréal Philippines launched a chatbot named Liv to provide customers with personalized beauty advice and product recommendations. Liv was able to ask customers questions about their skin type and preferences and then recommend the best L'Oréal products for their needs. The chatbot was integrated with Facebook Messenger and was able to handle high volumes of customer queries.

5. **AirAsia Philippines - AVA:** AirAsia Philippines launched a chatbot named AVA to provide customers with real-time flight updates and assist them with booking flights. AVA was able to handle customer queries about flight schedules, prices, and even book flights directly through Facebook Messenger. The

chatbot was integrated with AirAsia's existing booking system, resulting in faster booking times and increased customer satisfaction.

Overall, these chatbot-powered marketing campaigns were successful because they provided personalized customer service and made it easier for customers to make purchases or receive information. They also helped to generate leads by providing customers with relevant product recommendations and promotions.

## X. Video Marketing

### *What is video marketing and why is it important?*

Video marketing is the use of videos to promote and market a product or service. It involves creating and sharing videos that showcase your brand, products, or services, to reach and engage with your target audience.

Video marketing has become increasingly important in recent years, as it has been found to be one of the most effective forms of content marketing.

There are several reasons why video marketing is important:

1. **Increased engagement:** Videos have been found to be more engaging than text or images alone. They can capture people's attention and convey information in a more dynamic and interesting way, which can lead to higher engagement rates.

2. **Improved conversion rates:** Video marketing can also lead to improved conversion rates. Studies have shown that including a video on a landing page can increase conversion rates by up to 80%.

3. **Brand awareness:** Video marketing can help to increase brand awareness and recognition. It can be used to showcase your brand's values, products, or services in a way that is memorable and impactful.

4. **Increased reach:** Videos can be shared across multiple platforms and can reach a wider audience than other forms of content.

5. **Improved SEO:** Videos can also improve search engine optimization (SEO). Google and other search engines prioritize websites that have video content, which can help to boost your website's ranking in search results.

Overall, video marketing is a powerful tool for businesses looking to reach and engage with their target audience. It can be used in a variety of ways, such as product demos, explainer videos, testimonials, and more.

### How to create effective video marketing campaigns

Creating effective video marketing campaigns involves a series of steps, including planning, scripting, filming, editing, and promoting. Here's a more detailed breakdown:

1. **Define your goals:** Determine what you want to achieve with your video marketing campaign. Is it to generate leads, increase brand awareness, or drive

61

sales? Having a clear objective in mind will help you create more targeted content.

2. **Know your audience:** Identify your target audience and their preferences. What type of videos do they enjoy watching? What tone and style will resonate with them? Understanding your audience will help you create content that speaks directly to them.

3. **Develop a concept:** Once you have your goals and audience in mind, brainstorm concepts for your video. What story do you want to tell? How will you engage your audience and keep them interested? Consider using humor, storytelling, or other creative elements to capture your audience's attention.

4. **Scripting:** Once you have your concept, script your video. Make sure your script is clear, concise, and engaging. Consider hiring a professional scriptwriter or copywriter to help you craft the perfect message.

5. **Filming:** When it's time to film, make sure you have the right equipment and location. Use a high-quality camera and microphone to capture clear audio and visuals. If you're filming indoors, make sure the lighting is appropriate.

6. **Editing:** Once you've filmed your video, it's time to edit it. Use editing software to refine your footage, add special effects or music, and cut out any unnecessary

footage. Keep your video short and engaging, aiming for a length of around 1-2 minutes.

7. **Promotion:** Finally, promote your video on social media, email newsletters, and other channels. Encourage your audience to share your video with their friends and followers, and consider investing in paid promotion to reach a larger audience.

Overall, effective video marketing campaigns require careful planning, a clear message, high-quality visuals and sound, and strategic promotion. By following these steps, you can create compelling video content that resonates with your audience and achieves your marketing objectives.

*Examples of successful video marketing campaigns*

Here are some examples of successful video marketing international campaigns:

1. **Dollar Shave Club:** In 2012, Dollar Shave Club released a humorous, low-budget video that quickly went viral. The video, which featured the company's founder, Michael Dubin, explaining the benefits of the company's razor subscription service, helped to establish Dollar Shave Club as a major player in the razor industry. The video currently has over 27 million views on YouTube.

2. **Old Spice:** Old Spice launched a series of humorous and over-the-top commercials featuring the "Old Spice Guy," played by actor Isaiah Mustafa. The commercials, which debuted in 2010, were a hit with

63

audiences and helped to revitalize the Old Spice brand. The campaign was so successful that it spawned numerous parodies and even a response campaign featuring the "Old Spice Lady."

3.  **Nike:** Nike's "Just Do It" campaign, which began in the late 1980s, has become one of the most iconic ad campaigns of all time. The campaign features a series of motivational videos featuring famous athletes and everyday people pushing themselves to their limits. Nike has continued to use video marketing to great effect in the years since, releasing numerous inspiring and emotional ads that have resonated with viewers.

4.  **Airbnb:** Airbnb's "Live There" campaign, launched in 2016, aimed to encourage travelers to live like locals and experience the true essence of a destination. The campaign featured a series of short, documentary-style videos showcasing local neighborhoods and experiences. The videos were a hit with viewers and helped to establish Airbnb as a company that values authentic travel experiences.

5.  **Always:** Always' "Like a Girl" campaign, launched in 2014, aimed to combat the negative stereotypes surrounding girls and women. The campaign featured a video in which people were asked to demonstrate what it means to "run like a girl" or "throw like a girl." The video highlighted the harmful effects of gender stereotypes and went viral, sparking an important conversation about gender equality.

Here are 5 successful video marketing campaigns in the Philippines:

1.  **Jollibee's Kwentong Jollibee series:** Jollibee, a popular fast-food chain in the Philippines, launched a series of heartwarming videos that tell real-life love stories. These videos gained viral attention and became popular among Filipinos, resulting in increased brand awareness and emotional connection to the brand. The campaign showcased the importance of storytelling and emotions in creating effective video marketing campaigns.

2.  **Nestle's Chuckie "Magpakatotoo" campaign:** Nestle's Chuckie, a chocolate milk brand, launched a campaign that highlighted the importance of being true to oneself. The campaign included a series of videos featuring different people talking about their experiences of being true to themselves. This campaign resonated with the audience, especially the younger generation, resulting in increased brand awareness and loyalty.

3.  **McDonald's "Tuloy Pa Rin" campaign:** McDonald's Philippines launched a campaign that focused on the importance of being with loved ones during Christmas. The campaign included a heartwarming video featuring a grandfather and his grandson enjoying a meal together at McDonald's. This campaign struck an emotional chord with the

audience and resulted in increased brand awareness and engagement.

4. **Coca-Cola's "Taste the Feeling" campaign:** Coca-Cola launched a global campaign that emphasized the emotional experience of drinking Coke. The campaign included a series of videos that showcased different emotions associated with drinking Coke. The videos were highly engaging and resonated with the audience, resulting in increased brand awareness and emotional connection to the brand.

5. **Globe Telecom's "Create Courage" campaign:** Globe Telecom, a leading telecommunications company in the Philippines, launched a campaign that encouraged people to pursue their passions and dreams. The campaign included a video featuring an aspiring artist who overcomes her fears and pursues her dream. This campaign resonated with the audience, resulting in increased brand awareness and emotional connection to the brand.

Overall, these successful video marketing campaigns in the Philippines showcase the importance of emotions, storytelling, and authenticity in creating effective marketing campaigns that resonate with the audience.

## XI. Omnichannel Marketing

*What is omnichannel marketing and why is it important?*

Omnichannel marketing refers to the practice of providing a seamless and integrated customer experience across multiple channels and devices. It involves connecting various touchpoints that a customer might have with a brand and ensuring that each interaction is consistent and personalized. These touchpoints can include a brand's website, social media pages, physical stores, email marketing, mobile apps, and more.

The importance of omnichannel marketing lies in the fact that consumers today expect a consistent experience across all channels when interacting with a brand. They want to be able to switch between different devices and platforms without losing their progress, and they expect their data and preferences to be carried over. Brands that don't provide this seamless experience risk losing customers to competitors that do.

Omnichannel marketing also provides valuable data to marketers, allowing them to track customers' interactions with their brand and optimize their campaigns accordingly. By understanding how customers move between channels and what their preferences are, brands can deliver more targeted and personalized messaging and improve overall customer satisfaction.

In short, omnichannel marketing is important because it allows brands to deliver a consistent and personalized experience across all touchpoints, meeting the expectations of

67

modern consumers and providing valuable data for marketers to optimize their campaigns.

### How to create a seamless customer experience across multiple channels

Here are some tips on how to create a seamless customer experience across multiple channels:

1. **Understand your customers' needs and preferences:** The first step in creating a seamless omnichannel experience is to understand your customers' needs and preferences. You can use customer data to analyze their behavior, demographics, and preferences, and use this information to personalize your messaging and content across all channels.

2. **Consistent branding:** Your brand should have a consistent look, tone, and feel across all channels. This helps to reinforce your brand identity and build trust with customers.

3. **Cross-channel communication:** Your customers should be able to move seamlessly between channels without losing any information or context. For example, if a customer starts a conversation with a chatbot on your website, they should be able to continue the conversation on social media without having to repeat their question.

4. **Personalization:** Personalizing your messaging and content based on customer data is key to creating a seamless omnichannel experience. Use customer data to create targeted marketing campaigns, personalize email newsletters, and suggest relevant products or services.

5. **Mobile optimization:** With more and more customers using mobile devices to access content and make purchases, it's important to ensure that your website, emails, and other channels are optimized for mobile.

6. **Integration and synchronization:** To create a truly seamless omnichannel experience, all your channels should be integrated and synchronized. This means that customer data, purchase history, and other information should be shared across all channels, and that customers can access their information and complete transactions on any channel.

7. **Map out the customer journey:** Start by mapping out the customer journey across all channels, from the initial touchpoint to the final sale and beyond. Identify pain points and areas for improvement, and brainstorm ways to streamline the experience.

8. **Use data to personalize the experience:** Collect data on customer preferences, behaviors, and interactions across all channels. Use this data to personalize the experience and provide relevant content and offers.

9. **Integrate your technology stack:** To provide a seamless experience, your technology stack should be integrated across all channels. Use tools like customer relationship management (CRM) software to manage customer interactions and data, and ensure that your website, social media, email marketing, and other channels are all linked together.

10. **Provide consistent branding and messaging:** Your brand should be consistent across all channels, with a clear and cohesive message. Use the same logos, fonts, and colors, and ensure that your messaging is consistent across all channels. This will help build brand recognition and trust, and make it easier for customers to engage with your brand across multiple channels.

By following these tips, businesses can create a seamless omnichannel experience that meets the needs and preferences of their customers, builds brand loyalty, and ultimately drives sales and revenue.

### *Examples of successful omnichannel marketing campaigns*

Here are five examples of successful omnichannel marketing campaigns:

1. **Starbucks:** Starbucks is known for its successful omnichannel marketing campaigns. The company has created a seamless experience across its mobile app, online ordering, in-store experiences, and rewards program. Starbucks customers can order ahead and pay through the mobile app, earn rewards, and pick up

70

their order in-store or via drive-thru. The mobile app also allows customers to send digital gift cards to friends and family.

2. **Disney:** Disney has implemented an omnichannel marketing strategy by offering a seamless experience across its various properties, including theme parks, movies, merchandise, and digital channels. For example, customers can book a vacation package online, plan their itinerary through the My Disney Experience app, make dining reservations, and use MagicBands to access their hotel room and theme park tickets.

3. **Sephora:** Sephora has created a successful omnichannel marketing campaign by integrating its online store with its brick-and-mortar stores. The company has implemented features such as a virtual try-on tool that allows customers to test makeup and skincare products online, a loyalty program that rewards customers for purchases both in-store and online, and a personalized recommendation system that suggests products based on a customer's previous purchases and preferences.

4. **Nike:** Nike has created an omnichannel marketing campaign that seamlessly integrates its online store with its brick-and-mortar stores. The company has implemented features such as a Nike app that allows customers to reserve products online and pick them up in-store, as well as a personalized recommendation

system that suggests products based on a customer's browsing and purchase history. Nike has also implemented a loyalty program that rewards customers for purchases both in-store and online.

5. **Best Buy:** Best Buy has implemented an omnichannel marketing campaign that integrates its online store with its brick-and-mortar stores. The company has implemented features such as a "reserve online, pick up in-store" option that allows customers to purchase products online and pick them up at a local store, a personalized recommendation system that suggests products based on a customer's previous purchases and browsing history, and a loyalty program that rewards customers for purchases both in-store and online. Best Buy has also implemented a price match guarantee that allows customers to get the best price across all channels.

Here are five examples of successful omnichannel marketing campaigns in the Philippines:

1. **McDonald's Philippines - "McDo+Delivery"**
   McDonald's launched the McDo+Delivery campaign, which aims to make delivery orders easier and more convenient for customers. The campaign involved integrating all of the brand's channels, such as the website, mobile app, and social media platforms, to provide a seamless customer experience. Customers can place orders through any channel and track their delivery in real-time.

2. **Globe Telecom - "My Globe App"**

   Globe Telecom, one of the largest telecommunications providers in the Philippines, created the "My Globe App" to provide a seamless customer experience across all channels. The app allows customers to access and manage their accounts, view their bills, and purchase add-ons and promos. It also provides real-time customer support through chat, email, and phone.

3. **Lazada Philippines - "Shoppertainment Live"**

   Lazada, the largest online shopping platform in the Philippines, launched Shoppertainment Live, a live streaming show that combines shopping and entertainment. The show features product demonstrations, games, and performances by local celebrities. Customers can make purchases directly through the show's interactive chat function, providing a seamless and engaging shopping experience.

4. **The SM Store - "Call to Deliver"**

   The SM Store, a department store chain in the Philippines, launched the "Call to Deliver" campaign to provide customers with a safe and convenient shopping experience during the pandemic. Customers can place orders through the store's hotline or social media platforms and have their purchases delivered to their doorstep. The campaign also includes virtual shopping assistance, allowing customers to shop with the help of a personal shopper through video call.

5.  **Jollibee Foods Corporation - "Jollibee App"**
    Jollibee, a popular fast-food chain in the Philippines, created the Jollibee App to provide a seamless and convenient customer experience. The app allows customers to place orders, customize their meals, and track their delivery in real-time. It also provides exclusive deals and rewards for app users, encouraging customer loyalty.

## XII. Implementing Next Level Marketing Strategies

*How to develop a plan to implement next level marketing strategies in your own business*

Developing a plan to implement next level marketing strategies in your business requires careful planning and execution. The first step is to define your goals and objectives. What are you trying to achieve with your marketing efforts? Once you have a clear understanding of your goals, it is important to identify your target audience and understand their needs, preferences, and behaviors. This information will help you create a comprehensive marketing strategy that is tailored to your specific audience.

The next step is to choose the right marketing channels. This involves identifying the platforms and channels that are most effective in reaching your target audience. For example, if your target audience is primarily active on social media, you may want to focus your marketing efforts on platforms like Facebook, Instagram, or Twitter.

Once you have identified your marketing channels, it is time to develop your messaging and creative assets. Your messaging should be consistent across all channels and should speak to the needs and interests of your target audience. Your creative assets should be engaging, visually appealing, and aligned with your brand identity.

It is also important to measure the success of your marketing efforts. This requires the use of analytics tools and data tracking. You should regularly review your data and use it to make informed decisions about how to adjust and optimize your marketing strategy.

Finally, it is important to continuously iterate and improve your marketing strategy. This involves staying up to date with the latest marketing trends and technologies and being willing to adapt your strategy as needed. With a well-planned and executed next level marketing strategy, you can effectively reach your target audience, build brand awareness, and drive business growth.

### Best practices for integrating next level marketing into your overall marketing plan

Integrating next level marketing strategies into your overall marketing plan requires careful planning and execution.

Here are some best practices to keep in mind:

1. **Understand your audience:** To effectively implement next level marketing strategies, you need to have a deep understanding of your target audience. This

75

includes their demographics, behaviors, preferences, and pain points. Conduct market research and gather customer insights to inform your marketing approach.

2. **Define your goals:** Next, clearly define your marketing goals and how next level marketing strategies can help you achieve them. This could include increasing brand awareness, driving website traffic, generating leads, or improving customer engagement.

3. **Align with business objectives:** Ensure that your next level marketing strategies align with your overall business objectives. This means understanding how marketing can contribute to revenue and other key performance indicators.

4. **Create a cohesive brand message:** Develop a cohesive brand message that aligns with your marketing goals and resonates with your target audience. This message should be consistent across all channels, including social media, email marketing, and website content.

5. **Utilize multiple channels:** Next level marketing requires a multi-channel approach. This means utilizing a variety of channels, such as social media, email marketing, content marketing, influencer marketing, and paid advertising, to reach your target audience and achieve your marketing goals.

6. **Personalize your messaging**: Next level marketing requires personalization. This means tailoring your messaging and content to individual customer needs and preferences. Utilize customer data and behavior to create targeted messaging that speaks directly to their pain points and motivations.

7. **Continuously measure and optimize:** Finally, it's important to continuously measure and optimize your next level marketing efforts. This includes analyzing key metrics such as website traffic, engagement rates, and conversion rates to identify areas for improvement. Use this data to refine your marketing approach and achieve even better results over time.

*Tips for measuring the effectiveness of your next level marketing efforts*

Measuring the effectiveness of your next level marketing efforts is crucial to determining the success of your campaigns and making informed decisions for future strategies.

Here are some important tips for effectively measuring the impact of your next level marketing efforts:

1. **Define clear goals and KPIs:** Before launching any marketing campaign, it's important to clearly define your goals and the key performance indicators (KPIs) you will use to measure success. These KPIs could include metrics such as website traffic, social media engagement, email open rates, conversion rates, or revenue generated.

77

2. **Use analytics tools:** To track the performance of your marketing campaigns, you'll need to use analytics tools that can measure your KPIs. These tools can include Google Analytics for website traffic, social media analytics platforms for social media engagement, and email marketing software for email open rates and click-through rates.

3. **Monitor results in real-time:** It's important to monitor the performance of your marketing campaigns in real-time, so you can quickly adjust if needed. This can include tracking the number of clicks or conversions generated by your campaigns, or monitoring social media mentions and engagement.

4. **Use A/B testing:** A/B testing is a valuable tool for measuring the effectiveness of your marketing campaigns. This involves creating two versions of a campaign, such as an email or social media post, and testing them with different segments of your audience to see which version performs better.

5. **Continuously optimize your campaigns:** Based on the data and insights gathered from your analytics tools and A/B testing, it's important to continuously optimize your marketing campaigns. This could involve adjusting the messaging or visuals used in your campaigns, or targeting different audience segments based on performance data.

By following these tips and regularly measuring the effectiveness of your next level marketing efforts, you can make informed decisions to continuously improve your strategies and drive better results for your business.

**Summary Takeaways**

Next level marketing involves leveraging technology, data, and creativity to provide a seamless, personalized, and engaging customer experience across all channels. By adopting next level marketing strategies, businesses can achieve their marketing goals more efficiently and effectively.

To implement next level marketing successfully, businesses need to have a well-thought-out plan that considers their unique business needs, target audience, and available resources. The plan should include clear goals, a thorough analysis of the market and competition, a strategy for integrating different marketing channels, a plan for measuring effectiveness, and a system for continuous improvement. It's also essential to stay up to date with the latest marketing trends, technologies, and best practices to remain competitive and relevant.

Measuring the effectiveness of next level marketing efforts is crucial to optimizing marketing strategies and achieving business goals. The key performance indicators (KPIs) used to measure effectiveness will vary depending on the specific goals of the campaign. However, some common KPIs used in next level marketing include website traffic, engagement rates, conversion rates, customer satisfaction, and return on investment (ROI).

Regularly tracking and analyzing these metrics will provide insights into what's working and what needs improvement, allowing businesses to adjust their strategies accordingly and achieve better results. Next level marketing is an essential element of modern-day business strategy. By leveraging technology, data, and creativity, businesses can provide a personalized and engaging customer experience across all channels, resulting in better customer engagement, increased sales, and improved brand loyalty.

To succeed in next level marketing, businesses must develop a well-thought-out plan, stay up to date with the latest trends and best practices, and regularly measure and analyze the effectiveness of their efforts to optimize their strategies and achieve their goals.

www.ingramcontent.com/pod-product-compliance
Lightning Source LLC
Chambersburg PA
CBHW070749220526
45467CB00018B/1593